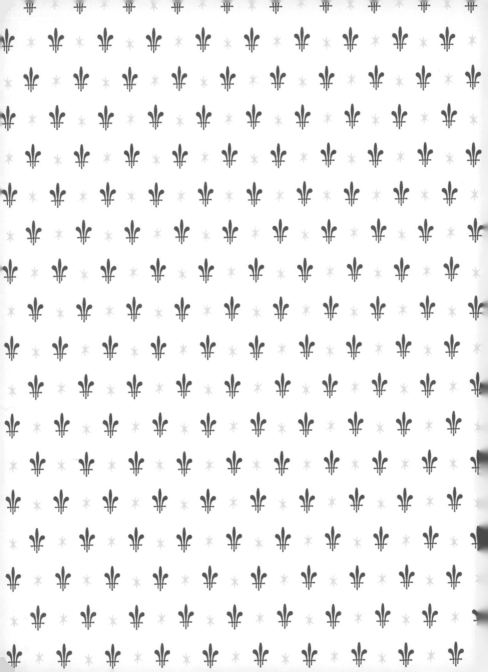

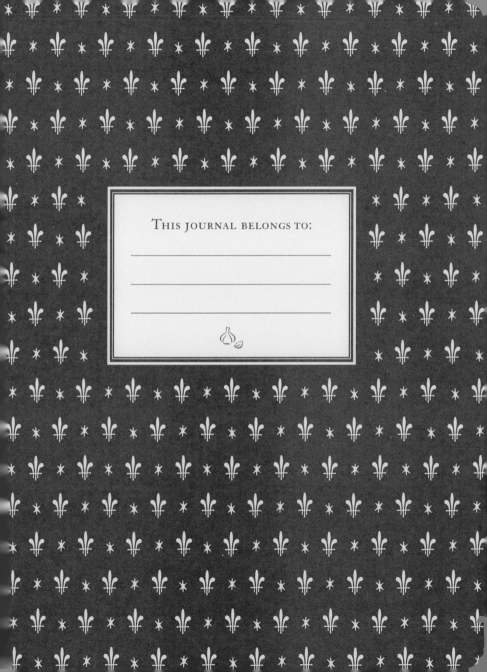

THIS JOURNAL BELONGS TO:

_____

_____

_____

DESIGN BY DOMINIKA DMYTROWSKI
PUBLISHED BY CLARKSON POTTER/PUBLISHERS,
RANDOM HOUSE, INC.
WWW.CLARKSONPOTTER.COM

Potter Style

Journal cover design courtesy of Alfred A. Knopf,
a division of Random House, Inc. From the first edition of the book
*Mastering the Art of French Cooking: The Only Cookbook That Explains
How to Create Authentic French Dishes in American Kitchens with American Foods*
by Julia Child, Louisette Bertholle, and Simone Beck.
Drawings by Sidonie Coryn. Copyright © 1961 by Alfred A. Knopf, Inc.
Published by Alfred A. Knopf, New York. Typography, binding, and jacket design
by Warren Chappell. Jacket illustrations by Sidonie Coryn.
Color illustration by Gigot Rôti. Photograph on the back by Paul Child.

Excerpted text from the Introduction by Judith Jones, copyright © 2001
by Alfred A. Knopf, a division of Random House, Inc., from
Mastering the Art of French Cooking, Volume One, Fortieth Anniversary Edition
by Julia Child, Louisette Bertholle, and Simone Beck.
Reprinted by permission of Alfred A. Knopf, a division of Random House, Inc.

PRINTED IN CHINA
ISBN 978-0-307-38192-7

THE STORY OF *"Mastering"* AT KNOPF

By Judith Jones

I N JUNE of 1960 a hefty manuscript—a treatise on French cooking by an American woman, Julia Child, and two French ladies, Simone Beck and Louisette Bertholle—landed on my desk. I had been an editor at Knopf for about three years, working primarily on translations of French books. But it was no secret that I had a passion for French cooking, so I was the logical person to read it.

The manuscript had been sent down from Cambridge by Avis de Voto, who worked as a scout for the Knopfs. She was the wife of the historian and writer Bernard de Voto, who had had a lively transatlantic correspondence with Julia on the subject of knives as a result of a piece he had done in *The Atlantic Monthly*. Avis soon became involved when she heard that Julia was working on a cookbook in Paris with Mesdames Beck and Bertholle, and she offered to try to find an American publisher. Her first submission met rejection, the publisher's comment being, Why would any American want to know this much about French cooking?

Well, it so happened that I did. As I turned the pages of this manuscript, I felt that my prayers had been answered. I had lived in Paris for three and a half years—at just about the same time the Childs were there, although our paths had never crossed—and most of what I learned then about cooking I absorbed from the butcher, the baker, the greengrocer, and the fishmonger. I would ask questions of them all, and then back in my tiny kitchen I would try to remember what the butcher's wife had told me about making frites or the poissonière about sautéing a dorade.

When I returned to the States, I realized how totally inadequate the few books that dealt with French food really were. They were simply compendiums of shorthand recipes and there was no effort to instruct the home cook. Techniques were not explained, proper ingredients were not discussed, and there was no indication in a recipe of what to expect and how to rectify mistakes. So the home cook, particularly an American home cook, was flying blind.

Yet here were all the answers. I pored over the recipe, for instance, for a beef stew and learned the right cuts of meat for braising, the correct fat to use (one that would not burn), the importance of drying the meat and browning it in batches, the secret of the herb bouquet, the value of sautéing the garnish of onions and mushrooms separately. I ran home to make the recipe—and my first bite told me that I had finally produced an authentic French boeuf bourguignon—as good as one I could get in Paris. This, I was convinced, was a revolutionary cookbook, and if I was so smitten, certainly others would be.

. . .

The rest is history. In the fall of 1961 we published *Mastering the Art of French Cooking* (incidentally, Alfred Knopf, when I told him the title we had settled on, said if anyone would buy a book by that title, he would eat his hat), and after Craig Claiborne pronounced the book a classic, the book went into a second printing before Christmas. Of course, when Julia went on television the following summer as the French Chef all of America fell in love with her. But everything she taught on camera was grounded in this seminal book—understand what you are cooking, do it with care, use the right ingredients and the proper equipment, and, above all, enjoy yourself.

JUDITH JONES
Senior Editor

—Excerpted from the Introduction to *Mastering the Art of French Cooking, Volume One, Fortieth Anniversary Edition*

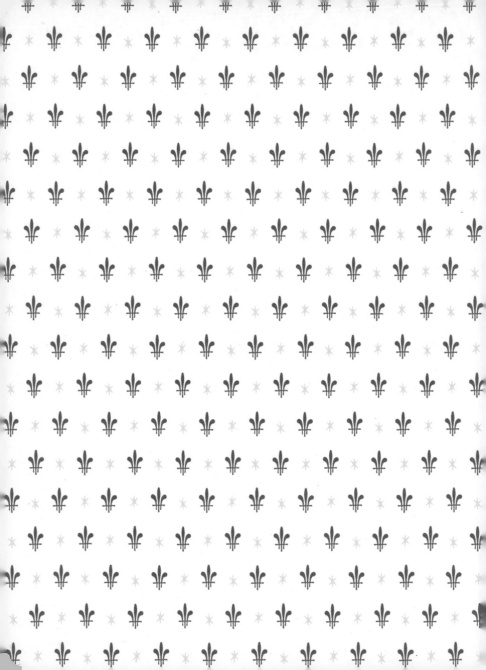